P9-EEO-425

FOR MY PARENTS, MY FIRST DINNER COMPANIONS AND STILL DAMN GOOD ONES.

AND FOR MY PARTNER IN ALL THINGS, LOUISE.

Many, many people have given freely of their time, energies, and ideas concerning this book.

I would like to thank Jo Lynne Lockley at the Chef's Professional Agency

for getting me out to San Francisco in the first place.

Jackie Kileen, my biggest fan and eventual editor, for believing in the book.

Fred Hill for nursing the book until it was sold and continuing to nurse me afterwards.

Bill LeBlond at Chronicle for ending up with two book contracts instead of one.

In Mexico, I would like to thank Patricia Quintana, Martha Chapa, Carmen Ortuna,

Alicia and Jorge de Angela for showing me the Mexico of creative food and generous people.

I would like to give special thanks to Soledad Diaz Allamirano

for her generosity and quick friendship.

GRACIAS

And, of course, Henry, for showing me Oaxaca's soul.

Thanks to Mark Miller, Jimmy Schmidt, Jonathan Waxman and Larry Forgionne

for showing me what great food was all about.

Thanks to the family and friends too numerous to mention in Texas and California

for making me realize what food means as communion.

Special thanks to Ward Robilliard and Andrea Jarrell

for believing in me and remaining good friends.

Thanks to Carl, Steven, Kit and Molly for believing in Marimba and making it a reality.

Thanks to my partners Kim and Tom for providing the energy in this busy year

to help make the food products a reality.

Thanks most of all to Louise Clement for her love and support.

MUSICA
FOR
YOUR
MOUTH

SALSA

BY REED HEARON

PHOTOGRAPHY
BY KAREN CAPUCILLI

BOOK DESIGN
BY CARBONE SMOLAN
ASSOCIATES

CHRONICLE BOOKS
SAN FRANCISCO

Text Copyright © 1993 by Reed Hearon.
Photographs Copyright © 1993 by Karen Capucilli.
All Rights reserved. No part of this book
may be reproduced in any form without written
permission from the publisher.

Library of Congress
Cataloging-in-Publication Data

Hearon, Reed
Salsa / by Reed Hearon:
photography by Karen Capucilli
p. cm.
ISBN 0-8118-0328-7
1. Salsas (Cookery) I. Capucilli, Karen II. Title
TX819.S29H43 1993
641.8' 14—dc20
92-25585
CIP

Food styling by Roscoe Betsill.
Printed in Hong Kong.

Distributed in Canada by Raincoast Books,
112 East Third Ave., Vancouver, B.C. V5T 1C8
10 9 8 7 6 5 4 3 2

Chronicle Books
275 Fifth Street
San Francisco, CA 94103

CONTENTS

6

INTRODUCTION

9

THE ORCHESTRATION OF SALSA
INGREDIENTS
TECHNIQUES
EQUIPMENT
SOURCES FOR INGREDIENTS

23

FIERY SALSA

43

MILD SALSA

59

MODERN SALSA

75

DESSERT SALSA

84

INDEX

WHEN I WAS A LITTLE BOY,

I USED TO GO TO A LITTLE HOLE-IN-THE-WALL RESTAURANT

WITH MY PARENTS TO EAT MEXICAN FOOD.

I REMEMBER LOVING MOST OF ALL THE STRANGE GREEN SAUCE

SALSA
MUSICA FOR YOUR MOUTH

THAT WAS ON THE CHICKEN ENCHILADAS.

SECOND BEST WAS THE SPICY RED SAUCE YOU ATE WITH THE CRISPY HOT CHIPS.

LATER ON WHEN I FIRST BEGAN TO LEARN ABOUT FOOD,

I FOUND OUT THAT THESE WERE BOTH SALSAS.

Growing up in central Texas, nearby Mexico seemed less exotic than faraway New York. By the time I was twelve, I had been as far as Mexico City three or four times. And San Antonio, that most Mexican of American cities, was an hour from our house. To me, Mexican food was what one ate as much as hamburgers or pizza.

Always fundamental to Mexican food for me was the salsa. It was what the Cajuns in Louisiana call "lagniappe" (something extra). Salsa was and is the difference between a boring steak and a feast I can't seem to get enough of. I have continued to travel throughout Mexico. And on each trip down I find a greater love for her people—and a few new salsas. I'm not suggesting that there is a direct relationship between the warm, easygoing generosity of Mexican hospitality and the spicy lagniappe of salsas. But I can't imagine a different sort of people creating the salsa

But what is a salsa? Salsa literally means "sauce" in Spanish. *Salsa bechemela* is white sauce, but thick bland white sauce is *not* what I think of when I hear the word *salsa*. Salsa is also a style of Latin music—a vibrant, rhythmic beat. Rhythm, beat; that sounds a little better. Seething, lively, hot, gotta-get-up-and-dance beat. Now we're talking!

So what does music have to do with food? Here, spoon some of this on that boring piece of chicken. Feel that happy, mouthfilling wow? Taste that gimme-some-more-of-that, boy-that's-great flavor? That's salsa! That's musica for your mouth!

Salsa is like food-music. But not just any kind of music. Salsa music. Spicy full-flavored food. Salsa livens up food. In Mexico, people have been perking things up with salsas since long before Columbus. And when Cortés and the Spaniards came, Mexicans discovered that salsas livened up all the Old World products like chicken, pork, beef, lamb, and cheese, too.

In this book you will find over thirty-seven recipes for salsas. Traditional. Fiery hot. Mild. Exotic. New. Very old. Even salsas for dessert. Cook these salsas. They are easy to make and fun, too. Once you master the simple technique of pan-roasting ingredients, you can make salsas out of almost anything. But remember, as with music, certain harmonies should be respected.

In preparing each of these salsas, I have adopted an ancient method appropriate for today. Before the Spaniards, there was very little cooking fat in the New World. So instead of frying all the ingredients, as is often done in Mexico, today, we will dry roast things in the old way. Cooked like this, salsas are not only great tasting, they are healthy too.

I hope you enjoy *Salsa* as much as I have. This is food that just can't help being fun. I know, I've enjoyed collecting these recipes and I sure have made friends cooking them. And, I still reach for the stuff every time I go to that (now not so little) hole-in-the-wall place in central Texas.

1
Anaheim

2
Avocado

3
Jalapeño
en Escabeche

4
Pasilla

5
Canela

6
Serrano

7
Ancho

8
Tomatillo

9
Caribe

10
Guajillo

11
Pequin

12
Morita

13
Arbol

14
Avocado Leaf

15
Jalapeño

16
Dried Cascabel

17
Poblano

18
Chipotle
en Adobo

19
Chipotle

20
New Mexican R

21
Habanero

I CAN REMEMBER FIFTEEN YEARS AGO IN AUSTIN,
POBLANO CHILES AND TAMARIND WERE IMPOSSIBLE TO FIND.
NOW I SEE THEM ALONGSIDE FRESH TORTILLAS AND CANNED *CHIPOTLES EN ADOBO*
IN MANHATTAN, PALM SPRINGS, SAN FRANCISCO, EVEN MINNEAPOLIS.
FOOD IS A CLEAR REFLECTION OF A CHANGING CULTURE.

THE ORCHESTRATION OF SALSA

HERE IS A SHORT LIST OF INGREDIENTS
I USE IN THIS BOOK. IF YOU CAN'T FIND SOMETHING, DON'T DESPAIR.
JUST BUG THE PRODUCE MAN AT YOUR GROCERY STORE;
PRETTY SOON EVERYTHING HERE WILL BE
AS COMMON AS CILANTRO.

AVOCADOS

Luscious, creamy avocados are the perfect counterpoint for hot chiles. Of the numerous varieties commonly available throughout the United States, the Hass variety is the most consistently ripe and flavorful. Look for dark, almost black, bumpy skins. If you find yourself with watery-tasting avocados (winter or non-Hass varieties), you can boost their flavor by mashing them with a tablespoon of avocado oil. Both lime juice and oil will also slow the discoloring of avocados, as will tightly covering cut surfaces with plastic wrap. For best results and flavor, however, prepare ingredients for a salsa using avocados ahead of time if you wish, but cut up your avocados at the last minute.

AVOCADO LEAVES

The fresh or dried leaves of the avocado tree have a wonderful anise-menthol flavor. You can sometimes find them in Latin American markets in the United States or, if you live in California or Florida, simply pick them off an avocado tree. Toast avocado leaves over an open flame until they release their powerful aroma. Leaves will keep dried up to six months or frozen up to two months.

CANELA

(MEXICAN SOFT-BARK CINNAMON)

The cinnamon widely used in Mexican cooking is called *canela*. It is the soft-bark variety of cinnamon you may remember from Red Hots candies as a child, not the hard-bark variety used in this country to flavor apple pie. Many large supermarkets have a section with little bags of Mexican chiles and spices hanging up on display. The cinnamon in these little bags is invariably canela. *There is no substitute.*

CHILES

Over one hundred different varieties of chiles exist in Mexico. Each one has its unique flavor and uses. When composing salsas, remember that while many chiles are hot, each one's flavor harmonizes uniquely well with certain foods. Chiles range from scorchingly hot habaneros and chipotles to mild Anaheims and sweet anchos. Individual types of chiles also vary widely in heat and flavor. The best rule is to taste chiles each time you buy them and adjust recipes accordingly. But remember, chiles add flavor and not just heat. If you cut back on the amount of chiles, you may end up with an insipid-tasting salsa. If you are sensitive to hot food, your best bet is to stick with the mild salsas in this book.

ANAHEIM

These are the fresh, long green chile most widely sold in this country. They tend to be a bit anemic in flavor, but they perk up when roasted and benefit from having their seeds kept in. Anaheims are 4 to 7 inches long and light green in color. They are widely available in the United States, but almost never seen in Mexico outside of the north.

ANCHO

The dried version of the red-ripe poblano chile, the ancho is perhaps the most widely used dried chile in Mexico. Measuring 3 to 5 inches long and 2 to 4 inches wide, the ancho is reddish brown in color and very wrinkled. But when held up to the light, an ancho chile is almost bright red. It is mild with sweet plum-raisin flavor. If you can find comparatively fresh ones (soft, not brittle), they are delightful eaten as is and can be used much like sun-dried tomatoes. This is a relatively easy dried chile to find in the United States, both in many large supermarkets (particularly in largely Mexican-American neighborhoods) and in most Latin American markets.

ARBOL

The small dried red *chile de árbol* is widely used in both Latin America and Southeast Asia. Arbol chiles are usually the dried ripe serrano, but sometimes árbols are made from cayenne chiles or even Thai chiles. Arbol chiles can vary widely in size (¾ inch to 3 inches long) and hotness with the smallest tending to be fiery indeed. They all have a pleasant, nutty-rich flavor when toasted and are often toasted then thrown whole into stews or sautés for flavor and a bit of heat. When ground or otherwise broken open, they are substantially hotter. Arbol chiles are widely available in many supermarkets. Spice Islands even packs them whole as "red chiles."

CARIBE

Caribe chile is crushed, dried red chile, made usually in this country from either the New Mexico type or the árbol type of chile. Caribe chile can vary widely in heat, depending on the chiles it was made from. The most commonly seen variety is packaged as "crushed red chile flakes" (what you see in pizza parlors). These are often stale in flavor. The freshest, most flavorful type is the crushed New Mexico *chile caribe* (the best is from Chimayo, New Mexico). Caribe chile is widely available in supermarkets and Latin American groceries. Caribe, like most dried chiles, improves when toasted.

CASCABEL

The round cascabel chile is the dried version of a Mexican chile (also called cascabel), which when ripe is similar in appearance to the Italian cherry pepper. Cascabels have a nutty-sweet flavor and loose seeds (hence cascabel or "rattle"). Rust-brown in color and about 1½ to 2 inches in diameter, the cascabel is often toasted whole in oil and added to soups. This chile is usually available only in Latin American markets. I have seen it in virtually every major metropolitan area in the United States.

CHIPOTLE (DRIED)

This is the dried version of a jalapeño varietal. The chipotle, along with the morita chile, is smoked over peat fires, which both add a wonderful flavor and allow thick-skinned chiles to dry before they rot. Chipotles can be very hot, but should not be underestimated from a flavor standpoint. Toast them before using in soups and salsas or even grind them in a spice mill as a wonderful seasoning. Chipotles are 2 to 4 inches in length and a light dusty brown in color. While the canned variety has become widely available (see below), the dried version is still hard to find, even in some Latin American markets. It is worth searching out for its incomparable flavor.

CHIPOTLE EN ADOBO

The chipotle chile (and, confusingly, the morita chile) is widely sold canned as *chile chipotle en adobo*. This is the dried chipotle chile (see above) simmered in salsa adobo and canned. It is delicious by itself as a condiment and may be used as you would Tabasco sauce. The smoky-sweet flavor varies with the packer (my favorite being the Herdez brand), but all versions are very hot. I see canned chipotles in more types of stores all the time. You should be able to find them in large supermarkets (particularly in a predominately Mexican neighborhood) or in most Latin American markets.

GUAJILLO

This is the dried form of the Mexican version of the New Mexico–type red chile. Also known as *mirasol* in Mexico, it's a reddish brown, smooth-skinned chile about 4 inches long. Its nutty-rich flavor is well suited to a wide range of salsas and *moles*. This chile is common in Latin American markets.

GUERO

The word *guero* means "pale" or "blond". This fresh chile is a pale, greenish blond in color and has a watery sharp flavor when raw. But when roasted, it takes on a rich flavor, more subtle and light than the roasted jalapeño. Guero chiles are 2½ to 4 inches long. I commonly see this chile in supermarkets in the western United States, often labeled as wax or banana pepper. Outside of the West, look in Latin American markets.

HABANERO

This fiery fresh chile is native to the Caribbean (*habanero* means "of Havana"), where it is known as the scotch bonnet. Its fierce heat is widely enjoyed in Mexico's Yucatán, where a little plate of the chiles in sour orange juice is a mealtime fixture. On the Scovil Heatness Index, the habanero is one thousand times hotter than the jalapeño, making it one of the world's two or three hottest chiles. (When I was chef at Corona Bar & Grill in San Francisco, one of

the cooks bet a dishwasher twenty dollars that he couldn't eat a whole habanero. The dishwasher calmly ate two whole chiles and returned to work. He called in sick the next day to much laughter all round.) The habanero's color ranges from pale green through bright yellow to orange. Its tremendous heat aside, the habanero has a wonderful pungent aroma and flavor. Habaneros are becoming more widely cultivated in the United States, but their fierce heat seems to doom the ultimate size of the market. A pound is a *lot* of peppers. Habaneros are available freeze dried (not very good) and in *salsa de habanero*, El Yucateco brand, which has a great flavor and is commonly available in Latin American markets.

JALAPEÑO

This fresh, dark green chile is the most widely eaten hot chile in the United States. Wonderful raw or roasted, its full, round flavor complements a wide range of foods. The familiar jalapeño is 2 to 3 inches long and best when it has a perfectly smooth skin and white seeds. Unfortunately, certain hybridized versions now on the market lack both heat and flavor. Fresh jalapeño chiles are usually sold in most large supermarkets.

JALAPEÑOS EN ESCABECHE

This is the familiar pickled jalapeño. The best-flavored brands are the ones in cans from Mexico (such as Herdez). Avoid brands with seeds removed. The pickling liquid from a can of jalapeños en escabeche has a great flavor of its own and makes an authentic addition to ceviches Canned jalapeños are very widely available.

MORITA

The morita chile is, like the chipotle, a smoked dried chile. The fresh chile is a red-ripe version of a small jalapeño grown near Morelia in the state of Michoacán. Also like the chipotle, the morita is very hot and smoky flavored, but it is much sweeter than the chipotle. The morita is small, 1 to $1\frac{1}{2}$ inches in length, and reddish in color. It is most commonly found in Latin American markets, often sold dried as chipotles or canned as *chiles chipotles en adobo*.

NEW MEXICO GREEN

This fresh (or rarely and wonderfully dried) chile is a variation of the same type grown as Anaheim chiles in California. Like its ripe version, the New Mexico red chile, the New Mexico green chile grows hot and full of flavor in the mountain air. The best varieties come from northern New Mexico and are mostly consumed on the pueblos there. I have had New Mexico green chiles that were hotter than jalapeños. Unfortunately, these chiles are infrequently seen in markets outside of New Mexico.

NEW MEXICO RED
(CHIMAYO)

I grew to love the toasty-rich flavor of this dried chile when I lived in Santa Fe. The best versions are grown in arid northern New Mexico on hillsides in and around the little town of Chimayo. In fact, the true Chimayo chiles are so prized for their flavor that aficionados will pay three to four times the price of regular New Mexico chiles in order to get the Chimayo. Much like grapevines, chile bushes grown on hillsides with just enough water to survive appear to produce fruits with a much more intense, complex flavor. The New Mexico chile varies from 3 inches for the Chimayo type to 8 inches for irrigated varieties from the south. The best chiles are hot, smoky sweet with nutty, bricky flavors. Many supermarkets and Latin American markets carry New Mexico chiles. Los Chileros de Santa Fe sells Chimayo chiles (see Sources for Ingredients at the end of this chapter).

PASILLA

The pasilla is a dried chile, 5 to 8 inches long and 1 inch wide, with blackish, wrinkled skin and a deep cocoa-like flavor. The name "pasilla," unfortunately, is sometimes used in this country for the fresh poblano chile or the dried mulato chile. The pasilla turns up all over Mexico not only in *moles*, but also in salsas, particularly salsas for fish. These chiles are easy to find in most Latin American markets, as long as you are aware of potential name confusion.

PEQUIN

In Spanish, *pequin* means "little" and these round, dried red chiles are indeed small; sometimes as many as twenty-five will fit in a tablespoon. Don't let their size fool you. Pequin chiles pack a wonderful sharp, sweet-nutty flavor, which is particularly suited to the grilled and stewed dishes of northern Mexico and south Texas. Pequin chiles are the wild progenitor of most of the chile family we use in this book, including the bell pepper. Pequins are easy to find; many supermarkets and virtually all Latin American food stores carry them.

POBLANO

This dark-green, cone-shaped fresh chile was virtually impossible to find in this country fifteen years ago, but now I see it in supermarkets across the country. No wonder. When roasted and peeled, its meaty, richly flavored flesh is indispensible to everything from chiles rellenos to salsa ranchera. Look for smooth-skinned chiles about 4 inches in length. These chiles (the fresh versions of anchos) are sometimes confusingly called pasillas.

SERRANO

This light-green, small chile is the essence of bright, clean heat. Indispensible to many fresh table salsas, the serrano is one of the easiest fresh chiles to find, usually turning up in supermarket produce cases. Look for chiles that are $1\frac{1}{2}$ to 3 inches long and $\frac{1}{2}$ inch wide with smooth skins and white seeds.

CILANTRO

Also known as coriander and Chinese parsley, cilantro is the most widely used fresh herb in the world, turning up in foods in virtually every major cuisine in either leaf or seed form. Yet its sprightly flavor seems controversial; many people find it soapy tasting. If you number among those people, don't give up on cilantro yet. Do what the people of the Yucatán do. Add a leaf or two of fresh mint to a few tablespoons of cilantro when you chop it. Cilantro is one of the few herbs whose stems are commonly chopped and eaten along with the leaves.

EPAZOTE

This powerful, almost medicinally flavored fresh herb is no doubt an acquired taste. But as someone who has very definitely acquired the taste for epazote, I will say its camphoric, almost kerosenelike flavor is indispensible in black bean dishes as well as in a wide range of fish and shellfish dishes. Epazote is appearing more and more in Latin American and specialty produce markets around the country, especially in the summertime. But your safest bet is to grow the hardy, bushy herb yourself.

GARLIC

Good fresh garlic is fundamental to great salsas. When you buy garlic look for hard, tight fresh heads. When you use garlic raw, be sure to cut each clove in half lengthwise and remove the greenish shoot that often grows through the middle of the clove. This shoot, when raw, adds an unpleasant, hot flavor to foods. The best garlic for Mexican foods is the red-skinned, small-cloved garlic found in the summertime. Its flavor is more pungently sweet and yet never sulfurous or off tasting. Buy garlic in stores that sell a lot of garlic.

LIMES

(KEY, MEXICAN, PERSIAN)

In the United States you never seem to get margaritas that taste as good as those in Mexico. Aside from the fact that cocktails always taste better on vacation, the reason is the limes. For obscure historical reasons we commonly eat the large Persian variety of lime, which is picked when bright green and underripe—a form that appeals to consumer preference as well as the desire of the produce industry for a fruit that ships easily. Unfortunately, underripe citrus fruits are dry and taste very sour. In addition, the Persian variety lacks the perfumy floral aroma of the Key (or Mexican) type. This lime, found in both the Florida Keys and Mexico, ranges from green to bright yellow on the outside, with a solid lemon color inside. Much smaller than the Persian lime, the Mexican lime's uneven coloration and small size usually bring a much lower price in United States markets than is commanded by Persian limes. So when you can find Mexican limes you should buy them—they taste better and cost less.

MEXICAN OREGANO

There are two varieties of oregano commonly sold dried in this country, Greek oregano and Mexican oregano. Greek oregano tastes like Mediterranean food, while Mexican oregano, naturally enough, tastes like Mexican food. Make sure the type you buy either is labeled "Mexican oregano" or is purchased in a Latin American market. Mexican oregano takes on its full complex flavor only after being toasted in a dry skillet until fragrant.

NOPALES

The nopal is the flat "leaf" or paddle of the prickly pear cactus. It is widely eaten throughout Latin America and the southwestern United States, where nopales are commonly seen in supermarkets. Look for small, pale-green, smooth leaves. The spines are easily trimmed off with a paring knife or swivel peeler.

ONIONS

When I mention onions in this book, I mean only the white type of medium-sized slicing onion. Do not substitute sweet or yellow onions.

PILONCILLO

These cones of raw sugar are commonly seen in Latin American markets. Piloncillo's very nutty and sophisticated flavor is almost rum-like. Unfortunately, these cones are a little cumbersome to use. They should either be grated or dissolved in boiling water before use.

PLANTAINS

The plantain is a starchy type of banana commonly eaten cooked as a vegetable. When its skin is yellow, it may be peeled and boiled like a potato. When you want a sweeter-flavored frying banana, select plantains that are almost solid black in color. Plantains like this are delicious simply browned on a griddle in a little oil and served with rice as a side dish.

TAMARIND

Tamarind is a dusky, light-brown seedpod native to Southeast Asia and widely appreciated throughout Latin America. The pulp around the seeds is commonly used as a flavoring in everything from Coca-Cola to Worcestershire sauce. To use the pulp, simply peel off the brittle wrappers and cover the seedpods with water. Simmer over medium-low heat until pulp loosens from seeds, about $\frac{1}{2}$ hour. Strain through a medium sieve and use resulting pulp to flavor salsas or beverages. Tamarind pods are widely available in supermarkets. Tamarind pulp is also available in both Latin American and Southeast Asian markets, but it tends to be stale and musty in flavor.

TOMATILLOS

Tomatillos are a bright-green to yellowish member of the gooseberry family. Like other gooseberries, they have a papery outer husk, which must be peeled off before using them. In addition, tomatillos should be rinsed in hot water to remove the sticky residue of the husks. Once cleaned, tomatillos are as versatile as tomatoes, good cooked as well as raw. Their tart astringent flavor balances richly flavored foods particularly well. Like most produce in the United States, tomatillos are picked under-ripe to facilitate shipping. When hard and green, their flavor can be acrid raw. Look for tomatillos that are slightly softer and have begun to take on a yellowish tinge. Smaller fruits seem to have better flavor, too. Tomatillos are available in most supermarkets. Canned tomatillos are also sold, but I cannot recommend them.

It is always a revelation to me when I go from California to Mexico, where tomatoes are meaty, ripe, and full of flavor. Fortunately, many of the salsas in this book call for pan-roasting tomatoes on a griddle or *comal* until black, a technique that wakes up the sad pale things found so often in American stores. Leave skins on. When tomatoes are not in peak season, it is best to look for the Roma variety, which at least are meaty. And when tomatoes are in full season, by all means, go to farmer's markets and buy a lot. The best solution to bad tomatoes is to not eat them.

WHEN I TEACH COOKING CLASSES, I ALWAYS LIKE TO POINT OUT
THAT WHILE MEXICAN FOOD MAY SEEM EXOTIC AND EVEN COMPLICATED,

TECHNIQUES

THE TECHNIQUES ARE IN FACT VERY SIMPLE, LOW-TECHNOLOGY SOLUTIONS.
CHARRING FOODS ON A GRIDDLE SEEMS TO DATE BACK TO CHARRING FOODS ON A HOT ROCK
NEXT TO A FIRE. ALL THE EASIER NOW THAT YOU CAN TURN THE FIRE ON AT THE FLIP OF A SWITCH.
ONE WORD OF CAUTION: WHEN PEELING FIERY CHILES, PEOPLE WITH SENSITIVE SKIN
SHOULD WEAR RUBBER GLOVES. IN ANY EVENT, BE CAREFUL ABOUT TOUCHING YOUR EYES
OR OTHER SENSITIVE FLESH AFTER HANDLING CHILES.

CHARRING AND PEELING FRESH CHILES

The easiest and best-tasting way to blister fresh chiles is to turn them over (or under) an open flame. My favorite method is to set the chiles on a metal grate over the open flame on my gas range. That way I can broil several chiles at once. It is also perfectly acceptable to broil chiles under a gas or electric broiler or even over a charcoal or gas grill. After I char chiles well all over, I place them in a small bowl and let them steam themselves as they cool. For best flavor, do not peel chiles under running water. Instead, rub off burnt peel with a cloth or paper towel. Don't worry if you leave an occasional fleck of charred peel, it will just add flavor to the dish.

PEELING AND SEEDING FRESH RAW CHILES AND BELL PEPPERS

To seed and devein fresh chiles and bell peppers, cut them in half lengthwise and scoop out any seeds or pith with the edge of a small spoon. You can peel fresh chiles and peppers without roasting them by cutting them in half lengthwise and then in half lengthwise again. Simply use a swivel-type vegetable peeler to peel away any tough (often waxy) skin from bell peppers and large chiles.

PAN-ROASTING DRIED CHILES, GARLIC, ONIONS, TOMATOES, AND TOMATILLOS

You can use any heavy-bottomed skillet, griddle, or a Mexican *comal* for pan-roasting. Simply put your skillet over low heat and arrange vegetables in a single layer. Do not add oil or salt or anything. When vegetables begin to cook and brown, turn them. Tomatoes should be cooked until a dark, brownish-black color. Vegetables are done when they are soft to the touch or can be pierced easily with a skewer, that's it. Although the technique is the same for most vegetables, the cooking time and advance preparation varies. Peel and cut onions into ½-inch slices to speed their cooking. Leave garlic unpeeled until after roasting. Wash tomatoes

EVERY MEDIUM AND LARGE AMERICAN CITY

I HAVE VISITED DURING THE LAST FIVE YEARS (UPWARDS OF TWENTY I'D GUESS)

SOURCES
FOR INGREDIENTS

HAS HAD AT LEAST ONE LATIN AMERICAN GROCERY LISTED IN THE PHONE BOOK.

IF YOUR LOCAL SUPERMARKET DOESN'T HAVE THE INGREDIENTS YOU'RE LOOKING FOR,

CHECK YOUR YELLOW PAGES AND CALL YOUR LOCAL LATIN AMERICAN MARKET.

IF THEY DON'T HAVE IT, CHANCES ARE THEY CAN GET IT FOR YOU.

IF YOU STILL HAVE TROUBLE FINDING SOME OF

THE SPECIAL MEXICAN PRODUCTS REQUIRED FOR THESE SALSAS, NEVER FEAR.

THERE ARE LOTS OF NICE FOLKS OUT THERE

WHO MAKE THEIR LIVINGS SOLVING JUST THAT PROBLEM.

SOME OF THEM ARE:

MARIMBA PRODUCTS

2317 Chestnut Street
San Francisco, CA 94123
Telephone: 415-776-1506 Fax: 415-391-9143
Catalog available.

I started this company because I was frustrated with the difficulty of finding some obscure Mexican products in San Francisco. We carry a full line of dried chiles, *hierba santa* and *epazote*, as well as a wide range of prepared table salsas, *recados* (marinades) and *moles*.

LOS CHILEROS DE NUEVO MEXICO

P. O. Box 6215
Santa Fe, NM 87502
Telephone: 505-471-6967
Catalog available.

These are really nice people who used to supply us with many of our chiles at Coyote Cafe. Their strong point is New Mexico food products, but they also carry a wide range of all types of dried chiles, as well as fresh New Mexico green chile in season and frozen green chile year round.

IT'S ABOUT THYME

P.O. Box 878
Manchaca, TX 78652
Telephone: 512-280-1192
Catalog available.

The town of Manchaca (pronounced *man-shack* by locals) is about ten miles from Austin where I grew up. These folks have a really amazing range of herbs in plant form which they ship by UPS all over the country. Buy some *hierba santa* and *epazote* from them.

LA PALMA

2884 24th Street
San Francisco, CA 94110
Telephone: 415-647-1500
No catalog available.

This is a terrific Mexican market in the tradition of barrio markets all across the United States. They will ship, but they are a little reluctant to do so. Drop in if you are in San Francisco for great handmade tortillas and *carnitas* on Saturday mornings.

TEXAS WILD GAME COOP

P.O. Box 530
Ingram, TX 78025
Telephone: 512-367-5875
Catalog available

I have been using the terrific game products from the folks in Ingram since the early 1980s. In the last few years, they have branched out from wholesaling to restaurants to retailing in grocery stores and catalog sales. Give them a call when you're in the mood for great venison, antelope, wild boar, game sausages, and of course, the best bacon.

Collecting salsa recipes in Mexico is a little like collecting
world views—everyone has one and everyone thinks that his or hers
is the authentic one. I like listening to people talk about themselves,
particularly their food. I have had salsa in the lean-to hut of
a mescal maker thirty miles down a dirt road in the wilds of Oaxaca
and I have had salsa in the company of a professor of gastronomy
in one of Mexico City's most exclusive restaurants.
Each of these salsas represents a long tradition reinvented,
like a fifty-year-old jazz tune played at two in the morning in a smoky club.

FIERY SALSA

Cooking is like music. There is no right way to do it,
but to do it well you must respect certain harmonies. The affinities of
quality raw materials for other foods is what makes cooking interesting.
Here is a sampling of fiery salsas I have eaten in my travels
throughout Mexico and the American Southwest.
Each one comes from a long tradition and reflects people and place.
All these salsas depend on fiery hot chiles for flavor.
You may reduce the amount of chile in any of these dishes,
but you will lose a great deal of flavor along with the heat.
Each of these packs a lot of flavor and tradition into a spoonful.
Try them all, they're terrific.

ALSO CALLED *SALSA CRUDA*, THIS IS THE MOST FAMILIAR OF THE TABLE SALSAS,

THE ONE MOST PEOPLE MEAN WHEN THEY SAY "SALSA."

SALSA FRESCA

DON'T STINT ON THE CHILES,

OR YOU WILL LOSE NOT JUST THEIR HEAT, BUT THE WONDERFUL FLAVOR.

THIS SALSA SEEMS POPULAR ON EVERYTHING FROM CHIPS TO TACOS TO BURGERS.

IT IS BEST THE DAY IT IS MADE.

3 serrano chiles

1 large ripe tomato

½ cup chopped white onion

1 teaspoon minced fresh cilantro

1 tablespoon olive oil

¼ teaspoon salt

¼ cup water

Chop together chiles with seeds and tomato using a knife or a food processor. Chop in onion and cilantro until a coarsely textured salsa is formed. Stir in oil, salt, and water.

Makes about 2 cups

Soledad is one of the nicest people I have met in my travels.
She is the delightfully generous chef-owner of one of Oaxaca's great restaurants, El Topil.

SALSA EL TOPIL

Soledad Diaz Altamiran has shared many of her secrets and a great deal of
her special mescal with me and my friends. When she serves her delicate quesadillas,
there is inevitably a bowl of this delicious salsa served alongside.
You must try her establishment, for the best *mole negro*, for the *sopa ranchera*,
for the violin player singing boleros on his homemade violin,
and best of all for Soledad.
This is my best recollection of her wonderful recipe.
It is worth trying to find the special Oaxacan type of pasilla chile;
it is smoked, reddish-black, and wrinkled.

In a heavy skillet over medium heat,
toast chiles until brown and fragrant,
about 3 minutes. Put unseeded chiles
and remaining ingredients in a blender.
Process at high speed until you have a
coarsely textured liquid.

Makes about 1½ cups

3 pasilla chiles,

preferably the Oaxacan kind

1 tomatillo,

husked, rinsed, and pan-roasted until
blistered, black, and soft

1 large ripe tomato,

pan-roasted until blistered, black, and soft

3 cloves garlic,

pan-roasted until brown and soft, then peeled

¼ teaspoon dried Mexican oregano,

toasted

¼ teaspoon salt

¾ cup water

If you love a spicy tomato salsa and find all those bottled *picante* salsas as insipid and canned-tasting as I do, try this wonderfully smoky, spicy tomato salsa.

CHARRED TOMATO TABLE SALSA

Pan-roasting the tomatoes makes even less-than-stellar, off-season tomatoes taste gutsy and rich. Don't be afraid of the black skins on the tomatoes and jalapeños. They are the key to this salsa's flavor. Wonderful on a wide range of foods and unbeatable with freshly made tortilla chips. This salsa will keep well for up to four days in the refrigerator, but its flavor is best if you let it warm to room temperature.

2 large ripe tomatoes,

pan-roasted until blistered, black, and soft

3 jalapeño chiles,

charred until blistered and black

1 small white onion,

thickly sliced and pan-roasted until dark brown and soft

2 cloves garlic,

pan-roasted until brown and soft, then peeled

¼ teaspoon dried Mexican oregano,

toasted

¼ teaspoon cumin seed,

toasted and then ground

½ cup water

Salt,

to taste

Chop together with a knife or food processor tomatoes, chiles with seeds, onion, and garlic until you have a coarsely textured salsa. Add oregano and cumin, thin with the water, and salt to taste.

Makes about 2½ cups

WONDERFUL

I'M NOT SURE I'D LIKE TO HAVE BEEN THE FIRST EUROPEAN TO TRY THIS FUNNY LITTLE "GROUNDNUT," WHICH IS NOT A NUT AT ALL, BUT A TUBER, LIKE A POTATO.

PEANUT SALSA

BUT MAYBE COLUMBUS (OR CORTÉS) FIRST TRIED THE PEANUT IN SOMETHING LIKE THIS SALSA, WITH ITS SURPRISING COMBINATION OF SMOKY CHIPOTLE CHILES, ROASTED GARLIC, AND TOMATO. ANY REACTION OTHER THAN LOVE AT FIRST BITE IS IMPOSSIBLE. PEANUTS AND PORK GO TOGETHER SO WELL I WISH I HAD BEEN AROUND FOR THEIR FIRST MEETING IN THE NEW WORLD. TRY SLOW ROASTING A LOIN OF PORK SLATHERED WITH THIS SALSA AND WRAPPED IN FOIL OR BANANA LEAVES. DELICIOUS. I BET PIGS AND PEANUTS WILL BE HANGING AROUND TOGETHER LONG AFTER COLUMBUS IS FORGOTTEN. THIS SALSA WILL KEEP WELL FOR TWO DAYS, BUT IS BEST IF THE NUTS ARE ADDED JUST BEFORE USING.

2 dried chipotle chiles

½ cup water

2 large ripe tomatoes,

pan-roasted until blistered, black, and soft, then chopped with skin

10 cloves garlic,

pan-roasted until brown and soft, peeled, and finely chopped

1 teaspoon finely ground canela

(Mexican cinnamon)

1 medium-sized white onion,

thickly sliced, pan-roasted until brown and soft, and coarsely chopped

2 whole cloves,

ground (large pinch freshly ground cloves)

¼ teaspoon salt

½ cup water

1 teaspoon finely chopped fresh marjoram

1 tablespoon olive oil

1 teaspoon freshly squeezed lime juice

⅓ cup chopped unsalted dry-roasted peanuts

In a heavy skillet over medium heat, toast chiles until brown and fragrant, about 3 minutes. Cool slightly, slit open, and remove seeds. In a large bowl, toss chiles with the water and let soak 10 minutes. In a blender, purée chiles with water. In a bowl mix together with remaining ingredients except peanuts. For best results, add peanuts to prepared salsa no more than 1 hour before serving.

Makes about 2¼ cups

I CAN ALREADY SEE SOMEONE LOOKING AT THIS RECIPE AND SAYING,

"NO WAY! TEN JALAPEÑOS, NOT FOR ME. NO SIR."

GRILLED JALAPEÑO SALSA

BUT WHEN YOU REMOVE THE SEEDS AND VEINS FROM THE CHILES,

YOU ARE LEFT WITH SOMETHING MUCH LESS HOT AND WONDERFULLY RICH AND FULL FLAVORED.

ROASTING THE VEGETABLES CAPTURES THE ESSENCE OF RANCH COOKING.

TRY THIS ON STEAKS, OF COURSE, BUT ALSO ON TUNA OR SWORDFISH.

OR FOR A DELIGHTFUL SOUP, STIR IT INTO BOILING BROTH AND GARNISH WITH LIME WEDGES,

DICED AVOCADO, AND TOMATO. KEEPS WELL FOR THREE DAYS IN THE REFRIGERATOR.

SERVE AT ROOM TEMPERATURE.

10 jalapeño chiles,

broiled or grilled, seeded, and coarsely chopped

1 medium-sized white onion, thickly sliced,

pan-roasted until brown and soft, and coarsely chopped

½ clove garlic,

finely chopped

1 tablespoon olive oil

½ teaspoon finely chopped fresh marjoram

¼ teaspoon salt

½ cup water

In a bowl mix together all ingredients.

Makes about 1½ cups

CASCABEL CHILES ARE THE DRIED RELATIVE OF THE ITALIAN CHERRY PEPPER.

I CALL THIS SALSA "RATTLESNAKE" BECAUSE IN SPANISH A RATTLESNAKE IS *SERPIENTE DE CASCABEL*.

RATTLESNAKE SALSA

WE ALSO USED TO SERVE IT IN THE VERY STYLISH GRILL ROOM AT THE NOW-DEFUNCT

RATTLESNAKE CLUB IN DENVER. THE COMBINATION OF TART TOMATILLOS, RICH TOMATO,

AND NUTTY SWEET CASCABEL CHILE IS DELIGHTFUL.

TRY IT WITH RICH FOODS LIKE DUCK OR GAME OR WITH WARM CHEESE.

KEEPS WELL UP TO FOUR DAYS IN THE REFRIGERATOR.

SERVE AT ROOM TEMPERATURE.

In a heavy skillet over medium heat,
toast chiles until brown and fragrant,
about 3 minutes.
Put unseeded chiles and remaining
ingredients in a blender
or food processor.
Process at high speed until you have
a slightly textured liquid.

Makes about 2¼ cups

3 cascabel chiles

2 tablespoons apple cider vinegar

1 large ripe tomato,

poached in water until soft

2 tomatillos,

husked, rinsed, and poached in water until soft

2 cloves garlic,

pan-roasted until brown and soft, then peeled

¼ teaspoon dried Mexican oregano,

toasted

1 whole clove,

ground (pinch freshly ground cloves)

¼ teaspoon salt

1 cup water

1 teaspoon olive oil

THIS SALSA IS CALLED "MOCHA" NOT BECAUSE IT HAS CHOCOLATE IN IT BUT BECAUSE OF ITS COLOR.

CHIPOTLE CHILES GIVE A RICH, SMOKY FLAVOR BALANCED BY THE NUTTY, SWEET FLAVOR

MOCHA SALSA

OF THE GUAJILLOS. MOCHA TRANSFORMS THE MOST ORDINARY FOODS INTO

SMOKY SOPHISTICATED DINING. I ENJOY IT ON ENCHILADAS, IN TAMALES, ON ANY BLAND WHITE MEAT,

SUCH AS CHICKEN OR PORK, OR WITH MELTED CHEESE IN A FRESH TORTILLA.

AND IT'S AWAYS POPULAR WITH CHIPS AT PARTIES.

KEEPS WELL FOR THREE DAYS IN THE REFRIGERATOR.

BEST AT ROOM TEMPERATURE.

2 guajillo chiles

2 canned chipotle chiles en adobo

2 tablespoons apple cider vinegar

1 large ripe tomato,
poached in water until soft

1 medium-sized white onion,
thickly sliced, pan-roasted until brown and soft

4 cloves garlic,
pan-roasted until brown and soft, then peeled

½ teaspoon ground canela
(Mexican cinnamon)

¼ teaspoon dried Mexican oregano,
toasted

1 whole clove,
ground (pinch freshly ground cloves)

¼ teaspoon salt

1 tablespoon sesame seeds,
toasted

1 tablespoon unsalted
dry-roasted peanuts

1 cup water

In a heavy skillet over medium heat,
toast guajillo chiles until
brown and fragrant, about 3 minutes.
Cool slightly, slit open, and
remove seeds and veins.
Put chiles and remaining ingredients
in a blender or food processor.
Process at high speed
until you have a slightly
textured liquid.
Sprinkle salsa with additional
sesame seeds, if desired.

Makes about 2¾ cups

SOPHISTICATED

PICO DE GALLO MEANS "BEAK OF THE ROOSTER."

EACH OF THE THREE POSSIBLE VERSIONS OF THIS SALSA HAS A SHARP BITE TO IT.

THREE BEAKS OF THE ROOSTER

MOST PEOPLE THINK OF TOMATOES IN PICO DE GALLO SALSA,

BUT IT'S GREAT WITHOUT THEM TOO, PARTICULARLY WHEN TOMATOES ARE OUT OF SEASON

OR FIGURE HEAVILY ELSEWHERE IN THE MEAL.

IT IS ALSO GREAT WITH AVOCADOS, IN ADDITION TO TOMATOES.

USE ON GRILLED MEATS OR IN TACOS OR TOSSED AT THE LAST MINUTE INTO SOUPS OR STEWS.

5 or 6 serrano chiles,

1 cup finely chopped red onion

¼ cup finely chopped fresh cilantro

¼ teaspoon salt

2 tablespoons water

1 teaspoon olive oil

1 medium-sized ripe tomato,
chopped (optional)

1 medium-sized ripe avocado,
diced (optional)

In a bowl mix together all ingredients.
Add avocado at the last minute, if using.

Makes 1 to 3 cups

GREAT

If I had to pick one of the most surprising and versatile salsas in the book,

this would be it. The tangy green flavor of the tomatillo

CHIPOTLE TOMATILLO SALSA

balances so nicely with the smoky richness of the chipotle peppers.

The great thing about salsas is that they zip up the taste of even boring dishes.

Try a chicken breast poached in this

(you can even pour some of this salsa over a chicken breast and microwave it).

Then put the cooked chicken inside a warm tortilla. Yum.

This salsa keeps well for three days in the refrigerator. Best at room temperature or hot.

2 dried chipotle chiles

or 5 morita chiles

1 cup hot water

6 tomatillos,

husked, rinsed, and pan-roasted until brown and soft

1 medium-sized white onion,

*thickly sliced, pan-roasted until brown and soft,
and coarsely chopped*

6 cloves garlic,

pan-roasted until brown and soft, then peeled

¼ cup chopped fresh cilantro

¼ teaspoon salt

*In a heavy skillet over medium heat,
toast chiles until brown and fragrant,
about 3 minutes. Cool slightly,
slit open, and remove seeds.
In a small bowl toss chiles with 1 cup of
the water and let soak for 10 minutes.
Put chiles, water, and remaining
ingredients in a blender.
Process at high speed until you have a
slightly textured liquid.*

Makes about 2½ cups

TANGY AND SMOKY

THESE TWO SALSAS ARE BOTH VERY HOT, BUT ALSO ABSOLUTELY DELICIOUS.

AND AS DIFFERENT AS NIGHT AND DAY. THE HABANERO CHILE SALSA IS A STAPLE OF THE YUCATÁN

WORLD'S HOTTEST SALSAS

AND IS BEST EATEN WITHIN AN HOUR OF MAKING IT; THE CITRUS-CHILE FLAVOR INTENSIFIES

TO SCREAMINGLY HOT THE LONGER IT SITS. THE ÁRBOL CHILE SALSA APPEALS

TO THE LEATHERY MEN OF THE RANCHES OF NORTHERN MEXICO AND SOUTH TEXAS.

SHARP AND BRICKY TASTING, IT KEEPS ALMOST INDEFINITELY AT ROOM TEMPERATURE.

I WILL NOT PRESUME TO TELL THE DEDICATED WHEN IT IS APPROPRIATE TO USE THESE SALSAS.

WORLD'S HOTTEST SALSA I

15 árbol chiles

2 tablespoons apple cider vinegar

3 cloves garlic,

pan-roasted until brown and soft, then peeled

¼ teaspoon cumin seed,

toasted and then ground

¼ teaspoon dried Mexican oregano,

toasted

½ teaspoon salt

1 cup water

*In a heavy skillet over medium heat,
toast chiles until brown and
fragrant, about 3 minutes. Put unseeded
chiles and remaining ingredients in a
blender or food processor.
Process at high speed until you have a
slightly textured liquid.*

Makes about 1½ cups

WORLD'S HOTTEST SALSA II

3 habanero chiles,

sliced into rings with seeds

¼ cup freshly squeezed orange juice

2 tablespoons freshly squeezed
lemon juice

¼ cup finely chopped red onion

*In a bowl mix together all ingredients.
Do not salt.*

Makes about 1 cup

SCREAMINGLY HOT

THIS IS A FIERY SALSA ALL RIGHT, BUT BOY DOES IT HAVE A GREAT FLAVOR.

I LOVE THIS WITH CHIPS, SCRAMBLED IN WITH EGGS, ON ROASTED CHICKEN OR FISH,

FIERY CHIPOTLE SALSA

OR WITH MELTED CHEESE. THE CHIPOTLE IS A VARIETY OF RIPE JALAPEÑO SMOKED OVER PEAT

TO DRY IT. TRY THIS SALSA WITH A SINGLE-MALT SCOTCH.

(I'M NOT KIDDING. FOOD-AND-BEVERAGE PAIRINGS PRODUCE SOME REAL SURPRISES!)

THIS SALSA WILL KEEP WELL UP TO FIVE DAYS IN THE REFRIGERATOR.

BEST SERVED AT ROOM TEMPERATURE.

3 dried chipotle chiles

1 cup hot water

1 medium-sized white onion,
thickly sliced, pan-roasted until brown and soft

8 cloves garlic,
pan-roasted until brown and soft, then peeled

1 tablespoon sherry vinegar

¼ teaspoon cumin seed,
toasted and then ground

¼ teaspoon dried Mexican oregano,
toasted

1 tablespoon olive oil

½ teaspoon salt

*In a heavy skillet over medium heat,
toast chiles until brown and fragrant,
about 3 minutes.
Cool slightly, slit open, and remove seeds.
Toss chiles with ½ cup of the water
and let soak for 10 minutes.
Combine chiles, soaking water,
and remaining ingredients in a blender.
Process at high speed until
you have a slightly textured liquid.
Add remaining ½ cup water.
Let cool if used as a table salsa.*

Makes about 2 cups

IN LITTLE TACO RESTAURANTS IN MEXICO AND THE SOUTHWESTERN UNITED STATES, VALUE AND FLAVOR ARE ALL THAT MATTERS. WITH AVOCADOS EXPENSIVE IN BOTH COUNTRIES,

TAQUERIA GUACAMOLE

IT IS NATURAL THAT AN ECONOMICAL SALSA EVOLVED TO STRETCH THE LUSCIOUS BUTTERY AVOCADO, SO WELL SUITED FOR GRILLED MEATS. THIS SALSA PACKS A TERRIFIC FLAVOR, AS WELL AS BEING BOTH LESS EXPENSIVE AND LOWER IN CALORIES THAN TRADITIONAL GUACAMOLES. DON'T STINT ON THE CHILES OR THE SALT; REMEMBER THERE IS A LOT OF WATER IN THIS SALSA. IT'S BEST WHEN MADE WITHIN AN HOUR OF USING AND WILL KEEP WELL COVERED FOR TWENTY-FOUR HOURS.

Put all ingredients except onion in a blender and process at high speed until smooth. Fold in onions, if using.

Makes about 2 ½ cups

1 large ripe avocado,

peeled and pitted

2 jalapeño chiles with seeds

¼ cup coarsely chopped fresh cilantro

1 clove garlic,

peeled

¼ teaspoon salt

1 cup water

2 teaspoons avocado oil or olive oil

¼ cup diced red onion,

(optional)

After a recent trip to Mexico, I fixed dinner for some friends
and their four-year-old Alex. I had made a *mole* from the Puebla area.
Alex was hungry, but I didn't think he would eat any of it.
To my surprise, Alex cleaned his plate and asked for more.
People are often surprised by the range of flavors present
in Mexican cooking, a subtlety that did not escape Alex.
The *mole* was rich and redolent of spices, but it was not hot.
Much of the cuisine is surprisingly mild. If you or your guests
are sensitive to hot foods, try the Pumpkin Seed Salsa in this section.
It is a suave sauce more reminiscent of Spanish or Italian cooking

MILD SALSA

than of macho chile cookoffs. Many people are unexposed
to the layered flavors present in authentic Mexican seasoning.
Heat is handled much as it is in classic Chinese banquets.
There is a rhythm of point and counterpoint, throughout the meal
and within individual dishes. What makes salsas work is counterpoint,
so please don't assume that just because you don't enjoy feeling that your
mouth is on fire, you won't enjoy salsas.
Each of the salsas in this section relies on chiles for flavor more than heat.
You will lose a lot of flavor if you change the quantity of chiles.
But do not fear.
None of these salsas will send you running to the water tap.

On weekends in central and south Texas, after a night of vigorous salsa dancing, bleary-eyed people flock to restaurants for a plate of huevos rancheros,

SALSA RANCHERA

the famous cure for what the Mexicans so aptly call *crudo*. One Austin restaurateur parlayed a particularly good version of salsa ranchera into a sizeable fortune by serving it on *everything*: steaks, chicken, enchiladas, pizzas, you name it. And he was right. This salsa seems to love everything and everybody. It keeps well for up to four days in the refrigerator. Warm it or serve it at room temperature.

1 jalapeño chile

2 small poblano chiles

2 large ripe tomatoes,

pan-roasted until blistered, black, and soft, then chopped with peel

1 medium-sized white onion,

thickly sliced, pan-roasted until brown and soft, then chopped

3 cloves garlic,

pan-roasted until brown and soft, then peeled and minced

¼ teaspoon cumin seed,

toasted and then ground

¼ teaspoon dried Mexican oregano,

toasted

¼ cup water

¼ teaspoon salt

1 teaspoon olive oil

Over a flame or under a broiler, char both kinds of chiles until blistered all over. Let chiles cool in a small bowl or in a paper bag. Peel, seed, devein, and chop poblano chiles. Chop jalapeño unpeeled with seeds. In a bowl mix together chopped chiles with remaining ingredients.

Makes 2 ½ cups

Guajillo chiles are the prehybrid version of the New Mexico and California types
of dried red chiles. Either of these could be a substitute, but they lack the smoky

GUAJILLO CHILE SALSA

intensity of the guajillo. This is the real version of that vinegary junk that
the Mexican fast-food places serve in the little pouches. And the real thing's great.
It makes a terrific table salsa on all kinds of foods or,
without the vinegar, becomes a fine red chile sauce for enchiladas and the like.
This salsa keeps well for five days in the refrigerator.
It is best served at room temperature or hot.

In a heavy skillet over medium heat,
toast chiles until brown
and fragrant, about 3 minutes.
Cool slightly, slit open,
and remove seeds and veins.
Put chiles and remaining ingredients
in a blender. Process at
high speed until you have
a slightly textured liquid.

Makes about 2 ¼ cups

4 guajillo or New Mexico red chiles

1 medium-sized tomato,

pan-roasted until blistered, black, and soft

¼ cup apple cider vinegar

(optional)

3 cloves garlic,

pan-roasted until brown and soft, then peeled

½ teaspoon dried Mexican oregano,

toasted

½ teaspoon cumin seed,

toasted and then ground

¼ teaspoon salt

¼ teaspoon freshly grated orange zest

1 cup water

½ cup finely chopped white onion

WHEN I WANT TO IMPRESS A FOOD WRITER IN ONE OF MY RESTAURANTS, THIS IS THE
KIND OF SALSA I LOVE TO SEND OUT; PERHAPS JUST WITH BROILED FRESH GOAT'S CHEESE

PUMPKIN SEED SALSA

AND SOME BABY GREENS. THIS IS MEXICAN FOOD AT ITS MOST SURPRISINGLY SOPHISTICATED.
THE SALSA IS NUTTY, GARLICKY, SWEET, AND HOT, BUT ELUSIVE. IT JUST TASTES GREAT.
TRY IT ON WINTER SQUASH THAT HAS BEEN ROASTED OR SLOWLY GRILLED.
THIS SALSA IS BEST USED THE FIRST DAY IT IS MADE.
SERVE WARM OR AT ROOM TEMPERATURE.

3 guero chiles,
charred until blistered and black, seeded, and deveined

1 medium-sized white onion,
thickly sliced and pan-roasted until brown and soft

8 cloves garlic,
pan-roasted until brown and soft, then peeled

1 large ripe tomato,
pan-roasted until blistered, black, and soft

¼ cup pumpkin seeds,
toasted in 1 tablespoon olive oil until puffed and brown

1 cup water

¼ teaspoon toasted Mexican oregano

¼ teaspoon salt

*In a blender or food processor,
purée ingredients together until
a chunky salsa is formed.*

Makes about 2 cups

ELUSIVE

ALSO KNOWN AS *SALSA BORRACHA*, THIS IS AN ESSENTIAL PART OF ONE OF THE MOST
PERFECT DISHES IN THE MEXICAN REPERTOIRE, *BARBACOA*. ON WEEKENDS

DRUNKEN SALSA

AT EL ARROYO IN MEXICO CITY, UPWARDS OF FIVE THOUSAND PEOPLE A DAY TURN OUT TO EAT
THE SUCCULENT WHOLE MARINATED LEGS OF LAMB WRAPPED IN MAGUEY CACTUS LEAVES
AND COOKED WITH COALS IN A TIGHTLY COVERED PIT.
THE MEAT EMERGES MELTINGLY TENDER, JUICY, AND REDOLENT OF SMOKY CACTUS.
IT IS SERVED UP WITH FRESHLY MADE TORTILLAS AND PLENTY OF DRUNKEN SALSA.
HERE I'VE SUBSTITUTED NOPALES FOR THE UNAVAILABLE PULQUE.
IT IS WONDERFUL WITH LAMB OR CHICKEN COOKED IN ALMOST ANY MANNER.
AND IT WILL KEEP WELL FOR THREE DAYS IN THE REFRIGERATOR.
SERVE AT ROOM TEMPERATURE.

4 pasilla chiles

1 nopal (cactus paddle),
cleaned of all thorns and diced to yield ½ cup

½ cup water

5 cloves garlic,
pan-roasted until brown and soft, then peeled

2 large ripe tomatoes,
pan-roasted until blistered, black, and soft

1 tablespoon tequila

2 tablespoons chopped white onion

¼ teaspoon salt

**3 tablespoons crumbled fresh
white cheese**
(Mexican *queso fresco* or fresh goat's cheese
or feta cheese)

*In a heavy skillet over medium heat,
toast chiles until brown and fragrant,
about 3 minutes. Cool slightly, slit open,
and remove seeds and veins,
reserving seeds from 2 of the chiles.
In a heavy skillet over medium heat,
toast reserved chile seeds until brown
and fragrant, about 2 minutes.
In a blender purée diced cactus
with the water until smooth.
Add roasted chiles, roasted seeds, garlic,
tomatoes, and tequila.
Process until you have a slightly
textured liquid. Stir in onion and salt.
Sprinkle cheese on top just before serving.*

Makes about 2¼ cups

I FIRST FELL IN LOVE WITH THIS SALSA IN SANTA FE WHEN
I WAS OPENING THE COYOTE CAFE THERE WITH MARK MILLER.

NEW MEXICO GREEN CHILE SALSA

ONE OF THE MOST MAGICAL SMELLS IN THE WORLD IS THE AUTUMN AROMA
OF ENTIRE BUSHELS OF LOCAL GREEN CHILES
BEING ROASTED IN GIANT SQUIRREL-CAGE CHILE ROASTERS IN FRONT
OF THE MARKETS OF SANTA FE. THIS SALSA REMINDS ME OF THOSE CHILES AND OF SANTA FE.
IF YOU ARE LUCKY ENOUGH TO FIND NEW MEXICO GREEN CHILES,
BY ALL MEANS USE THEM. THEY ARE VERY SPECIAL. THIS SALSA IS A MULTIPURPOSE TABLE SALSA,
WHICH IS GREAT ON A WIDE RANGE OF FOODS. TRY STIRRING GENEROUS AMOUNTS OF IT
INTO PORK STEWING WITH POTATOES. KEEPS WELL FOR THREE DAYS IN THE REFRIGERATOR.
BEST SERVED HOT OR AT ROOM TEMPERATURE.

Place charred chiles in a small bowl
or paper bag to cool.
Peel, but do not seed.
In a food processor or with a knife,
chop together chiles with
tomato, tomatillos, onion, and garlic.
Transfer to a bowl
and stir in oregano, salt, and water.

Makes about 2 ¼ cups

**4 New Mexico green chiles or
Anaheim chiles,**

charred until blistered

1 medium-sized ripe tomato,

pan-roasted until blistered, black, and soft

2 tomatillos,

husked, rinsed, and pan-roasted until blistered,
black, and soft

½ cup chopped pan-roasted onion

2 cloves garlic,

pan-roasted until brown and soft, then peeled

¼ teaspoon dried Mexican oregano,

toasted

¼ teaspoon salt

1 cup water

THIS DELIGHTFUL SALSA, PERFUMED BY AVOCADO LEAVES, COMES FROM TEPOZTECO, A VILLAGE NEAR AN IMPORTANT AZTEC MONUMENT OUTSIDE OF CUERNAVACA.

SALSA TEPOZTECO

AVOCADO LEAVES ARE A LITTLE EXOTIC AND OFTEN HARD TO FIND, BUT THEY HAVE A WONDERFUL, TOASTY ANISE AROMA AND FLAVOR. YOU SOMETIMES SEE THEM DRIED IN SOME LATIN AMERICAN MARKETS OR YOU CAN PICK THEM OFF A TREE IN YOUR BACKYARD IF YOU LIVE IN AVOCADO COUNTRY. IF YOU CAN'T FIND AVOCADO LEAVES, TOASTED FENNEL SEED GIVES A SIMILAR FLAVOR. THIS SALSA IS JUST RIGHT FOR GRILLED OYSTERS OR SHRIMP. IT SHOULD BE USED THE SAME DAY IT IS MADE. BEST SERVED AT ROOM TEMPERATURE.

1 avocado leaf or
½ teaspoon fennel seed,

toasted and then ground

3 serrano chiles

1 small clove garlic,

peeled

10 tomatillos,

husked and rinsed

¼ cup finely chopped white onion

¼ teaspoon salt

If using avocado leaf, toast it over an open flame until fragrant. In a blender or food processor, purée avocado leaf or fennel with unseeded chiles, garlic, and tomatillos. Fold in diced onion and salt.

Makes about 1½ cups

DELIGHTFUL

CAMPECHE IS SECOND ONLY TO VERACRUZ IN ITS FAME FOR SEAFOOD.
HERE I RECENTLY ATE A STUNNING LUNCH OF A SPICY CRAB SOUP AND A WHOLE,

CAMPECHE SALSA

INCREDIBLY FRESH GROUPER FRIED AND TOPPED WITH A PARSLEY-LADEN
MOJO DE AJO (GARLIC SAUCE) THAT WAS AS GOOD AS ANY I HAVE EVER HAD.
IT WAS SERVED WITH FRESH TORTILLAS AND A BOWL OF THIS SALSA.
I WAS REMINDED ONCE AGAIN HOW PERFECT THE SIMPLE ACT OF EATING CAN BE.
THIS SALSA IS MADE WITH SOUR ORANGES, WHICH ARE VERY HARD TO FIND IN THE UNITED STATES.
I HAVE SUBSTITUTED A MIXTURE OF ORANGE, GRAPEFRUIT, AND LEMON JUICES.
IT IS MORE THAN SATISFACTORY BUT NOT THE SAME—MUCH LIKE EATING GROUPER
IN SAN FRANCISCO. THIS SALSA IS BEST THE DAY IT IS MADE.
SERVE IT AT ROOM TEMPERATURE.

5 pasilla chiles

3 cloves garlic,

pan-roasted until brown and soft,
then peeled and minced

1 cup fresh sour orange juice,

or ½ cup each freshly squeezed orange juice and red
grapefruit juice and the juice of ½ lemon

½ teaspoon salt

In a heavy skillet over medium heat,
toast chiles until brown
and fragrant, about 3 minutes.
Cool slightly, slit open,
and remove seeds. Crumble chiles
into a bowl and stir
in remaining ingredients.
Let sit for at least ½ hour before using.

Makes about 1½ cups

My friend Carmen is from the Mexico City suburb of Coyoacán, the home of the painter Frida Kahlo, among others. This is an old, bohemian artist's neighborhood,

CARMEN'S SALSA

which still retains its colonial charm in spite of being now surrounded by twenty million people. Carmen makes a wonderful dish of eggs scrambled with this salsa and strips of blanched nopales (cactus "leaves" or paddles). Not very hot, a touch sweet, and opulently flavorful, this salsa is also wonderful on poached chicken breasts. Keeps well up to five days in the refrigerator. Best served hot.

In a heavy skillet over medium heat,
toast chiles until brown
and fragrant, about 3 minutes.
Cool slightly, slit open,
and remove seeds.
In a small saucepan bring to a boil
vinegar, piloncillo, and water.
Add chiles and simmer until
sugar dissolves and chiles soften,
about 5 minutes. Let cool.
Combine with remaining ingredients in
a blender and purée until smooth.

3 ancho chiles

2 tablespoons apple cider vinegar

**1 small cone piloncillo
(Mexican raw sugar)**

or 3 tablespoons dark brown sugar

1 cup water

½ medium-sized white onion,

thickly sliced and pan-roasted until dark brown and soft

3 cloves garlic,

pan-roasted until brown and soft, then peeled

¼ teaspoon salt

Makes about 1¼ cups

Guacamole has become so common in the United States that most people do not think of it as a salsa. In fact, it is a pre-Hispanic dish of noble heritage.

GUACAMOLE

This is my favorite guacamole. It is unusual in that the tomato is roasted and allowed to cool before being mashed up with the other ingredients. Guacamole does not keep well and is best eaten right after being made. If you are making this for a party, you could prepare most of the ingredients in advance and mix them with the avocado at the last minute. If you add a tablespoon of olive oil or avocado oil to the guacamole and press plastic wrap onto its surface, it will keep up to three hours without discoloring, but will not taste quite as fresh. Guacamole is of course great with chips and the like, but try it like a compound butter on warm grilled or broiled meats and fish.

2 medium-sized ripe avocados

1 small ripe tomato,
roasted until blistered, black, and soft, then cooled

1 jalapeño chile,
diced with seeds

1 tablespoon minced white onion

2 teaspoons minced fresh cilantro

¼ teaspoon salt

In a bowl mash together avocado, tomato, and chile with the back of a fork until chunky smooth.
Stir in remaining ingredients.

Makes about 1½ cups

REED'S FAVORITE

THIS IS ANOTHER UNUSUAL GUACAMOLE, WHICH INCLUDES TOMATILLOS.
THE PLEASANTLY ACIDIC TOMATILLO NICELY BALANCES THE RICHNESS OF THE AVOCADO.

GUACAMOLE VERDE

AND WITH THE PRICE OF AVOCADOS THESE DAYS, THIS SALSA IS A GREAT WAY TO STRETCH THEM.
(THE NEXT TIME YOU HEAR AN AMERICAN POLITICIAN SPOUTING OFF IN FAVOR OF FREE TRADE,
REMEMBER OUR TRADE BARRIERS ENSURE THAT AVOCADOS ARE FIVE TIMES THE PRICE HERE
AS IN MEXICO). TRY THIS SALSA GENTLY HEATED OVER A SHRIMP ENCHILADA.
THIS KEEPS BETTER THAN MOST GUACAMOLES, BUT IS STILL BEST THE DAY IT IS MADE.

5 tomatillos,
husked and rinsed

½ clove garlic,
peeled

1 ripe avocado,
peeled and pitted

¼ cup minced fresh cilantro

2 teaspoons chopped fresh marjoram

3 serrano chiles,
minced with seeds

¼ cup minced white onion
(optional)

1 tablespoon olive oil

¼ teaspoon salt

1 cup water
or more as desired

*In a blender or food processor,
purée tomatillos and garlic.
Add avocado, cilantro, and marjoram
and purée until smooth.
Fold in remaining ingredients and
water to thin
(the salsa should be pourable).*

Makes about 2½ cups

THIS SPICY GREEN SALSA OF COOKED TOMATILLOS IS GREAT ON GRILLED MEATS OF ALL TYPES.
COMBINE IT WITH POACHED CHICKEN

SALSA VERDE

AND YOU HAVE ONE OF THE GREAT DISHES OF THE MEXICAN CUISINE.

NO WONDER IT IS ONE OF THE MOST COMMONLY USED SALSAS IN MEXICO.

WHENEVER YOU USE TOMATILLOS, LOOK FOR YELLOWISH OR SLIGHTLY SOFT ONES; THEY ARE RIPE

AND DO NOT HAVE THE SOMETIMES ACRID FLAVOR OF VERY HARD, BRIGHT-GREEN TOMATILLOS.

THIS SALSA WILL KEEP WELL FOR THREE DAYS IN THE REFRIGERATOR.

SERVE HOT OR AT ROOM TEMPERATURE.

*In a blender or food processor,
purée all ingredients except onion.
Fold in onion.*

10 tomatillos

husked, rinsed, and poached in water until soft

2 serrano chiles with seeds

¼ cup coarsely chopped fresh cilantro

½ cup water

¼ teaspoon salt

¼ cup finely diced white onion

Makes about 2 ½ cups

I had the privilege of working with some very talented American chefs in the early days, cooking what became fashionably labeled as southwestern food. Although I think, from an historical perspective, that southwestern food will be seen as part of the American assimilation of a new wave of Mexican immigration, there was nevertheless some very tasty food cooked in those years.

Salsas are a special category of foods.

I find it impossible to look at them without seeing

MODERN SALSA

their improvisational character.

Yet they are like haiku poetry or jazz saxophone; there are rules, even when you are breaking all the rules. Here are some of my favorite salsas from the modern era. I have eaten countless creations in the last few years that didn't work, and I will admit to some hesitation when it came time to retest some of my recipes in this section. But they're great. And a lot of fun to make. Try your hand at a few. Make up your own. But please, respect the food. There is plenty of great real food out there without wasabi, peach, and sun-dried tomato salsa.

THIS IS THE FIRST OF TWO SALSAS IN THIS BOOK DESIGNED FOR THE BACKYARD BARBECUE. I LOVE TO GRILL AND I LOVE THE IDEA OF BEING ABLE TO MAKE SALSA RIGHT ON THE GRILL

GRILLED PINEAPPLE SALSA

ALONG WITH WHATEVER I'M GRILLING. THIS SALSA IS FIERY, SMOKY SWEET AND ALTOGETHER DELICIOUS. PARTICULARLY GOOD WITH GRILLED PORK OR WHITE FISH, SPICED UP BEFORE GRILLING WITH SALSA ADOBO. LEFTOVERS KEEP WELL IN THE REFRIGERATOR FOR UP TO THREE DAYS. SERVE HOT OFF THE GRILL OR AT ROOM TEMPERATURE.

2 slices (¾ inch) peeled and cored
fresh ripe pineapple

2 Anaheim chiles

1 jalapeño chile

2 medium slices (½ inch) white onion

1 teaspoon olive oil

In a bowl toss pineapple, chiles, and
onion slices in the oil.
Grill over a wood or charcoal fire
until soft and richly browned,
about 10 minutes.
Pull tops off chiles and purée
all ingredients together
in a food processor or blender.

Makes about 2 cups

One of the things I love most about grilling outside is that you don't need to make a mess in the kitchen. This salsa was created just for outdoor cooking.

GRILLED TOMATO PEPPER SALSA

In northern Mexico you will often see cooks at vast grills cooking improbable numbers of chickens, whole kid, and great slabs of beef. Often onions, chiles, and other things join the meats on the grill. In this contemporary version, we grill tomatoes, sweet peppers, jalapeños, and onion together to create the perfect accompaniment for grilled foods. This salsa keeps well up to four days in the refrigerator. Serve it hot or at room temperature.

In a bowl toss tomato, bell peppers, onion slice, and jalapeños in the oil. Grill over a wood or charcoal fire until vegetables are soft and richly browned, about 10 minutes.
Pull tops off the jalapeños and bell peppers and purée them with all other ingredients in a food processor or blender.

1 medium-sized ripe tomato

1 small red bell pepper

1 small yellow bell pepper

1 thick slice (¾ inch) white onion

2 jalapeño chiles

1 teaspoon olive oil

1 tablespoon chopped fresh marjoram

¼ teaspoon salt

Makes about 2 cups

MANGOS ARE LIKE GREAT BIG PEACHES THAT SPENT THE SUMMER ON A TROPICAL ISLAND.
AS WITH MANY FRUITS, IT IS HARD TO IMPROVE ON THEIR NATURAL PERFECTION.

MANGO SALSA

BUT ANYTIME YOU WANT AN UNMISTAKABLE TROPICAL FLAVOR TO FOOD, TRY THIS SALSA ON
GRILLED PORK, SHRIMP, OR CHICKEN; MIXED WITH CRAB MEAT; OR ON RAW TUNA.
THIS SALSA WILL KEEP WELL IN THE REFRIGERATOR FOR ONE DAY.
GOOD COLD OR AT ROOM TEMPERATURE.

1 serrano chile,
minced with seeds

1 mango,
peeled, seeded, and diced

2 tablespoons fresh tamarind pulp

1 slice white onion,
pan-roasted until dark brown and soft, then diced

1 clove garlic,
*pan-roasted until brown and soft,
then peeled and minced*

1 tablespoon minced, fresh cilantro

½ cup diced raw red bell pepper
peeled, seeded, and deveined

In a bowl mix together all ingredients.

Makes about 2 cups

NATURAL PERFECTION

IN AUGUST, THE HEIGHT OF TOMATO SEASON IN THE SAN FRANCISCO BAY AREA,

FARMERS FROM SONOMA AND NAPA TRY TO OUTDO EACH OTHER, SEEING WHO CAN GROW

TOY BOX TOMATO SALSA

THE WILDEST SELECTION OF EXOTIC TOMATO VARIETIES. YOU SEE EVERYTHING

FROM CURRANT TOMATOES THE SIZE OF A PEA TO GIANT STARBURST TOMATOES,

BIGGER THAN A SOFTBALL, WHICH REVEAL A STARBURST OF ORANGE OR GREEN AGAINST A

RED BACKGROUND WHEN CUT OPEN. ONE GROWER I KNOW PACKS WHAT HE CALLS TOY BOXES,

A STAGGERING SELECTION OF DIFFERENT TOMATO TYPES.

THIS SALSA WAS CREATED TO SHOWCASE THE SUMMER'S FINEST SMALL TOMATOES.

BEST ABOUT A HALF HOUR AFTER BEING MADE.

NEVER REFRIGERATE FRESH TOMATOES.

$1/4$ cup sliced leek,

white part only

2 tablespoons water

1 teaspoon olive oil

2 cups mixed yellow and red
baby tomatoes,

stemmed and halved

3 tomatillos,

husked, rinsed, and diced

1 serrano chile,

minced with seeds

$1\frac{1}{2}$ teaspoons minced fresh lemon
thyme or basil or summer savory

1 teaspoon freshly squeezed lime juice

1 teaspoon sherry vinegar

$1/4$ teaspoon salt

*In a small skillet over low heat,
"sweat" leeks in the water and olive oil
until tender. Do not let brown.
Cool and mix together with other
ingredients in a bowl.*

Makes about $2\frac{1}{3}$ cups

SHOWCASE

THIS IS A SALSA I FIRST MADE ABOUT SIX YEARS AGO AND STILL LIKE VERY MUCH.
IT COMBINES THE MEATY FLAVOR OF BLACK BEANS WITH THE BRIGHT ACCENT

BLACK BEAN SALSA

OF FRESH POMEGRANATE JUICE. JUST SQUEEZE POMEGRANATES AS YOU WOULD AN ORANGE.
TAKE A PERFECTLY GRILLED CHICKEN BREAST, PUT IT ON TOP OF A PLATE FULL OF THIS SALSA,
AND TOP IT WITH A SLIGHTLY WARMED SLICE OF FRESH GOAT'S CHEESE. YUM.
THIS SALSA SHOULD BE SERVED WARM ON THE DAY IT IS MADE.

1 poblano chile,

charred until blistered

2 cups cooked black beans,

rinsed

2 tablespoons fresh pomegranate juice

(see Note)

**¼ cup *each* diced
raw red and yellow bell peppers**

peeled, seeded, and deveined

2 cloves garlic,

*pan-roasted until brown and soft,
then peeled and chopped*

1 thick slice (¾ inch) white onion,

pan-roasted until brown and soft, then chopped

**1 tablespoon diced canned chipotle
chiles en adobo**

1 tablespoon chopped fresh cilantro

¼ teaspoon cumin seed,

toasted then ground

Salt,

to taste

*Put poblano chile in a small bowl or a
paper bag and let cool.
Peel, seed, devein, and dice chile.
Put in a bowl and mix together chiles
with remaining ingredients.
Salt to taste.*

Makes about 2½ cups

*Note:
Bottled pomegranate juice tastes
old and stale, but—surprisingly—frozen
cranberry juice cocktail mix
is a good substitute.*

YUM

THIS RECIPE WAS MY FIRST PUBLISHED; *THE NEW YORK TIMES* RAN IT IN 1986.
MY FAVORITE WAY OF COOKING CORN IS TO ROAST IT IN THE HUSK,

ROASTED CORN SALSA

WHERE IT STEAMS IN ITS OWN JUICES. TRY IT LIKE THIS SPRINKLED WITH RED CHILE POWDER
AND LIME JUICE. THIS SALSA IS VERY VERSATILE, GOING PARTICULARLY WELL
WITH RICHLY FLAVORED FOODS, LIKE GOAT'S CHEESE, SAUSAGE, BEEF,
OR EVEN GRILLED OYSTERS. IF YOU INCREASE THE CORN TO EIGHT EARS,
YOU CAN USE THIS AS A SUAVE SIDE DISH. BEST SERVED AT ROOM TEMPERATURE
OR HOT WITHIN A FEW HOURS OF MAKING IT.

3 ears corn,

in their husks

1 tablespoon olive oil

½ cup diced, charred red bell pepper

(peeled, seeded, and deveined)

1 poblano chile,

charred, peeled, seeded, deveined, and diced

3 sun-dried tomatoes,

chopped

1 clove garlic,

*pan-roasted until brown and soft,
then peeled and chopped*

1 tablespoon minced fresh cilantro

**¼ cup chopped sautéed fresh wild
mushrooms (about ¼ pound)**

**1 teaspoon minced canned chipotle
chiles en adobo**

Salt,

to taste

*Preheat oven to 500°F.
Place corn in its husk
directly on oven rack for 5 minutes.
Remove and let cool.
Shuck corn and brush with olive oil.
Grill or broil corn
until it is caramel brown all over,
about 5 minutes. Cut kernels from the cob,
being careful not to cut into
woody part of cob. In a bowl mix corn
with remaining ingredients.*

Makes about 2 cups.

SUAVE

WHEN I WAS TESTING THE RECIPES FOR THIS BOOK, THE FAMOUS MONTEREY FOODS
PRODUCE MARKET IN BERKELEY HAD SOME FRAGRANT EARLY-SEASON MOREL MUSHROOMS.

WILD MUSHROOM SALSA

I COULDN'T RESIST. THIS SALSA IS A DREAM ON A WELL-AGED RIB STEAK
GRILLED OVER MESQUITE. TRY IT ALSO WITH WARM GOAT'S CHEESE IN A TORTILLA,
TOSSED WITH BABY LETTUCES IN A SALAD, OR JUST WITH CHIPS.
I RECOMMEND THAT YOU EAT THIS SALSA SOON AFTER MAKING IT, BUT IF YOU MAKE TOO MUCH,
IT WILL KEEP A DAY OR TWO IN THE REFRIGERATOR. SERVE HOT OR AT ROOM TEMPERATURE.
BY THE WAY, THE BEST BACON IN THE COUNTRY IS AVAILABLE FROM
TEXAS WILD GAME COOP IN INGRAM, TEXAS. IT IS MADE FROM LOCAL WILD BOARS.

**1 tablespoon diced pancetta
or quality smoked bacon**

**¼ pound fresh morels
or other wild mushroom,**

1 tablespoon chopped fresh cilantro

1 serrano chile,

minced with seeds

⅛ teaspoon salt

**1 tablespoon finely chopped
white onion**

*In a skillet over medium-low heat,
sauté bacon until cooked through,
but not brown, about 5 minutes.
Add mushrooms, raise heat to medium
high, and sauté, stirring often,
until mushrooms are soft, wilted, and
lightly browned, about 6 minutes.
Transfer mushroom mixture to a bowl,
add remaining ingredients,
and toss together.*

Makes about 1 cup

A DREAM

THIS SALSA REMINDS ME AGAIN OF HOW GREAT CONTRAST IS IN FOOD.

SWEET, ACID PINEAPPLE WITH RICH, SPICY, SMOKY CHIPOTLE.

PINEAPPLE CHIPOTLE SALSA

MY FRIENDS TOM WORTHINGTON AND PAUL JOHNSON OWN THE WEST COAST'S BEST

FISH COMPANY, MONTEREY FISH IN SAN FRANCISCO. THEIR CLIENT LIST READS

LIKE A *WHO'S WHO* OF RESTAURANTS IN CALIFORNIA (CHEZ PANISSE, SPAGO, SQUARE ONE).

SO PAUL AND TOM KNOW FISH. TOM IS ALSO A GREAT COOK AND LOVES TO GRILL

THE LOCAL CHILE-PEPPER ROCKFISH WITH HIS SECRET BARBECUE BASTE.

HE TOPS IT OFF WITH THIS SALSA. BEST SERVED AT ROOM TEMPERATURE

WITHIN A COUPLE OF HOURS OF BEING MADE.

**1½ cups finely diced
fresh ripe pineapple**

**1 tablespoon minced canned
chipotle chiles en adobo**

½ cup diced raw red bell pepper

peeled, seeded, and deveined

2 leaves epazote or 4 leaves fresh mint,

minced

2 teaspoons minced fresh chives

*In a bowl mix together all ingredients.
Do not salt.*

Makes about 2 cups

I FIRST MADE THIS FUNNY LITTLE SALSA IN TEXAS YEARS AGO WHEN

I WAS CATERING A PARTY FOR SOME UNIVERSITY OF TEXAS CELEBRITIES

JALAPEÑO BRAVO SALSA

AND THE PERSON I SENT OUT TO SHOP BOUGHT CANNED INSTEAD OF FRESH JALAPEÑOS.

THERE WAS ONE NOTORIOUS POLITICIAN PRESENT WHO WAS FAMOUS FOR DRINKING LOTS

OF SCOTCH, HATING LIBERALS, AND LIKING *HOT* FOOD.

I COULD NOT PASS UP THE OPPORTUNITY TO PLEASE SOMEONE WHO WAS

OTHERWISE KNOWN TO BE DIFFICULT TO REACH AN ACCORD WITH.

SO I TOSSED THE JALAPEÑOS—LIQUID AND ALL—IN A BLENDER WITH SOME CILANTRO,

THINNED IT OUT WITH WATER, AND FOLDED IN SOME CHOPPED ONION.

IN SPITE OF MY LONG HAIR, I MADE A NEW FRIEND THAT DAY. AND I DISCOVERED THIS SALSA,

WHICH CONTINUES TO BE ONE OF MY FAVORITES. IT IS *HOT*. BEST THE DAY IT IS MADE.

USE IT IN ANYTHING FROM BLOODY MARYS TO SCRAMBLED EGGS.

*Put unseeded chiles along with
their liquid and cilantro in a blender.
Process at high speed until you have
a slightly textured liquid.
Stir in chopped onion and the water.*

**1 can (8 ounces) jalapeño chiles
en escabeche**

1 small bunch cilantro

¼ cup chopped white onion

1 cup water

Makes about 2 cups

When it was first suggested that I add a dessert section to this book, I was intrigued. While the southwestern food movement had its share of ancho-chocolate this and cayenne-melon that, I was excited about making some simple chile-free salsas or condiments that would perk up otherwise boring desserts. Most of these salsas are based on classic flavor combinations. I have suggested a few ways to use each of these salsas,

DESSERT SALSA

not the least of which is just spooned on top of good vanilla ice cream. When seasonal fruits are at their peak, let your imagination run wild. Mix three kinds of berries with lemon zest and a scraped vanilla bean, or pair halved fresh cherries with shaved bitter chocolate and kirsch, or combine Fredricksburg peaches with bourbon, brown sugar, and toasted salted pecans or . . . You get the idea.

EVERYONE LOVES CHOCOLATE. ESPECIALLY WITH MINT, WITH NUTS, WITH BANANAS.

WHY NOT MIX THEM ALL TOGETHER IN AN EASY-TO-MAKE FUN LITTLE SALSA

CHOCOLATE PISTACHIO MINT SALSA

TO JAZZ UP CAKES, ICE CREAMS, OR EVEN COOKIE DOUGHS?

THIS SALSA IS BEST USED THE DAY IT IS MADE. SERVE AT ROOM TEMPERATURE.

YOU CAN GET TWO VERY DIFFERENT EFFECTS: SUAVE AND RICH FROM A PREMIUM

EUROPEAN CHOCOLATE SUCH AS TOBLER OR LINDT, OR SPICY AND CRUNCHY

FROM A QUALITY MEXICAN CHOCOLATE SUCH AS THOSE FROM OAXACA.

½ cup chopped
Swiss or Mexican chocolate

½ cup chopped
unsalted toasted pistachio nuts

1 medium-sized ripe banana,

peeled and diced

1 teaspoon minced fresh mint

*In a bowl gently mix together
all ingredients*

Makes 2 cups

My great-grandmother Amelia Rose had a fig tree in her backyard in San Antonio.

I have loved figs since I was big enough to climb that tree to get them.

FIG AND PISTACHIO SALSA

This recipe works well with dried figs and best with fresh figs (just leave out the water).

Any way you make it, enjoy this salsa spooned over cake or

ice cream (honey ice cream!). Keeps well up to three days in the refrigerator

as long as you add the pistachios at the last minute.

Best served warm.

In a bowl toss figs with boiling water.
Let sit for 10 minutes until figs plump.
Add remaining ingredients
and mix well.

1 cup diced dried Calimyrna figs
(top cut off)

¼ cup boiling water

2 tablespoons freshly squeezed
lemon juice

1 teaspoon freshly grated orange zest

1 tablespoon honey

¼ cup chopped
toasted unsalted pistachio nuts

Makes about 1½ cups

A year or so ago, I subjected my dear friend Louise to a road trip from
the city of Oaxaca to Puerto Escondido on the coast. She bravely rode for six hours

TROPICAL SALSA

in a Volkswagen Beetle on a winding, narrow, pothole-filled road
over high mountain passes and through thick jungle. I can safely say
that what Louise enjoyed most about the trip (after getting out of the car at the end)
was the abundance of tropical fruits we saw. We literally drove over and through
piles of mangos and mammeys that had fallen from trees.
I know of no better way to enjoy tropical fruits than to make a salsa like this
and sit down on a hot day with a bowl of homemade vanilla ice cream.
You can keep this salsa for a day in the refrigerator,
but better yet, fold it into softened ice cream and refreeze it.
Serve fruit at room temperature.

½ cup chopped ripe mango

½ cup chopped ripe papaya

¼ cup chopped ripe pineapple

½ cup chopped ripe banana

Pulp from 2 passionfruits, with seeds

1 tablespoon freshly squeezed lime juice

2 tablespoons freshly squeezed
orange juice

2 fresh mint leaves,
minced

In a bowl mix together all ingredients.

Makes about 2 cups

DELICIOUS

BANANAS AND RUM JUST *SOUND* SO GOOD TOGETHER.

IN THIS SALSA RECIPE WE BROIL THE BANANAS UNTIL THEY ARE CARAMEL COLORED

BANANA RUM SALSA

AND TOSS THEM WITH DARK RUM, A BIT OF BUTTER, AND CINNAMON.

I DON'T KNOW ANYONE WHO CAN RESIST THIS COMBINATION SPOONED WARM OVER

GOOD VANILLA ICE CREAM. IF YOU HAVE ANY LEFTOVER SALSA,

IT CAN BE REHEATED THE NEXT DAY.

2 medium-sized ripe bananas,

peeled and halved lengthwise

2 tablespoons sugar

2 tablespoons Meyer's dark rum

2 teaspoons butter,

softened

½ teaspoon ground canela

(Mexican cinnamon)

½ teaspoon vanilla extract

*Lay bananas out in a single layer
on a baking sheet.
Sprinkle with sugar and broil under
a hot broiler until brown and bubbly,
about 8 minutes.
Chop together, and transfer to a bowl.
Add rum, butter, canela, and vanilla
and mix well.*

Makes about 1 cup

IRRESISTIBLE

I LIKE THE OLD-FASHIONED FLAVORS YOU GET FROM PRESERVED FOODS.

AND THERE IS NO BETTER WAY TO ENJOY PEAK-OF-SEASON FRUIT ALL YEAR LONG THAN WITH

SIX-MONTH SALSA WITH RUM

THIS SALSA. YOU SIMPLY LAYER FRUITS IN STERILE GLASS JARS

(STERILIZE THEM IN YOUR DISHWASHER) AND TOP THEM OFF WITH RUM AND SUGAR.

SIT BACK AND LET TIME WORK ITS MAGIC.

I HAVE ONE FRIEND WHO MAKES THIS WITH FOUR TIMES AS MUCH RUM AND THEN USES

THE FLAVORED RUM TO MAKE COCKTAILS. BUT THAT'S ANOTHER BOOK.

SPOON THIS OVER POUND CAKE OR ICE CREAM OR SERVE IT WARMED OVER CHEESE BLINTZES.

WILL KEEP UP TO SIX MONTHS IN THE REFRIGERATOR.

2 cups Meyer's dark rum

2 cups Lemon Heart Demerara rum

2 cups piloncillo

(Mexican raw sugar) or dark brown sugar

1 large ripe pineapple,

peeled, cored, and cut into chunks

1 vanilla bean,

split

4 large mangos,

peeled, seeded, and cut into chunks

4 guavas,

peeled and cut into chunks

In a large pitcher mix both rums with
the sugar. In a sterilized 1-gallon glass
jar or crock, press the pineapple and
vanilla bean into a single layer.
Cover with 1/3 of the rum mixture.
Add mangos in a second layer and top
with another 1/3 of the rum.
Top off with guavas and pour remaining
rum over fruit. Press fruit down gently
to make sure it is submerged.
Cover jar or crock loosely. Salsa may be
kept up to 6 months in the refrigerator.
Best eaten after at least 1 week.

Makes about 3 quarts

MAGIC

INDEX

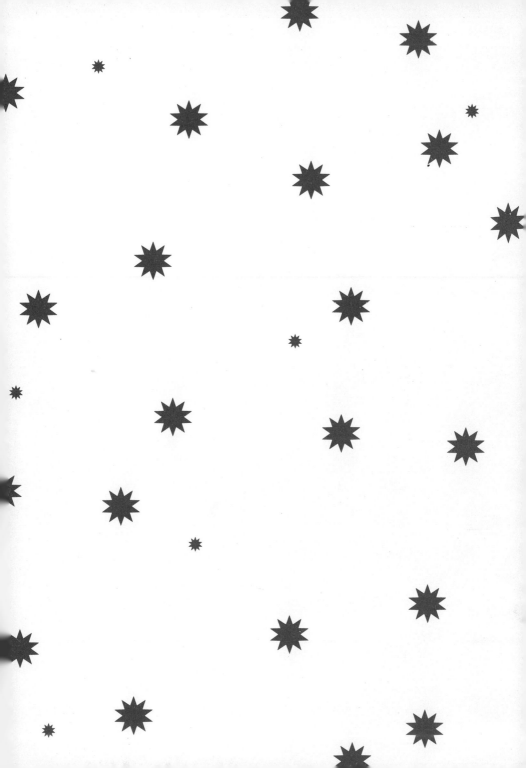

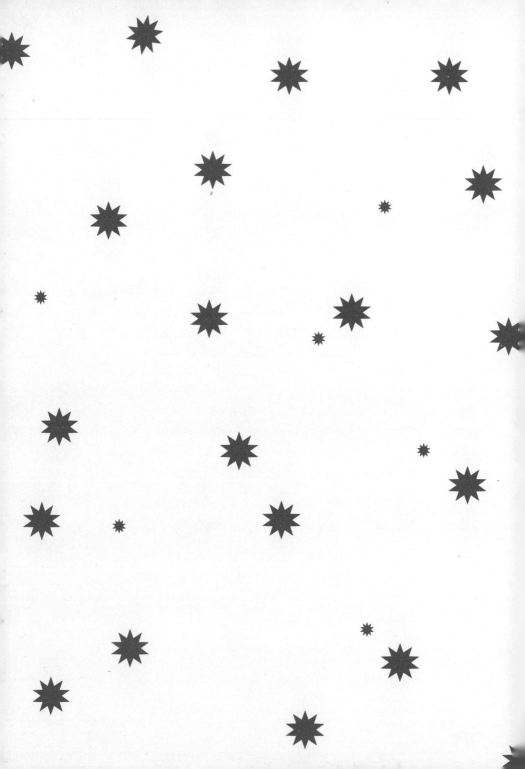